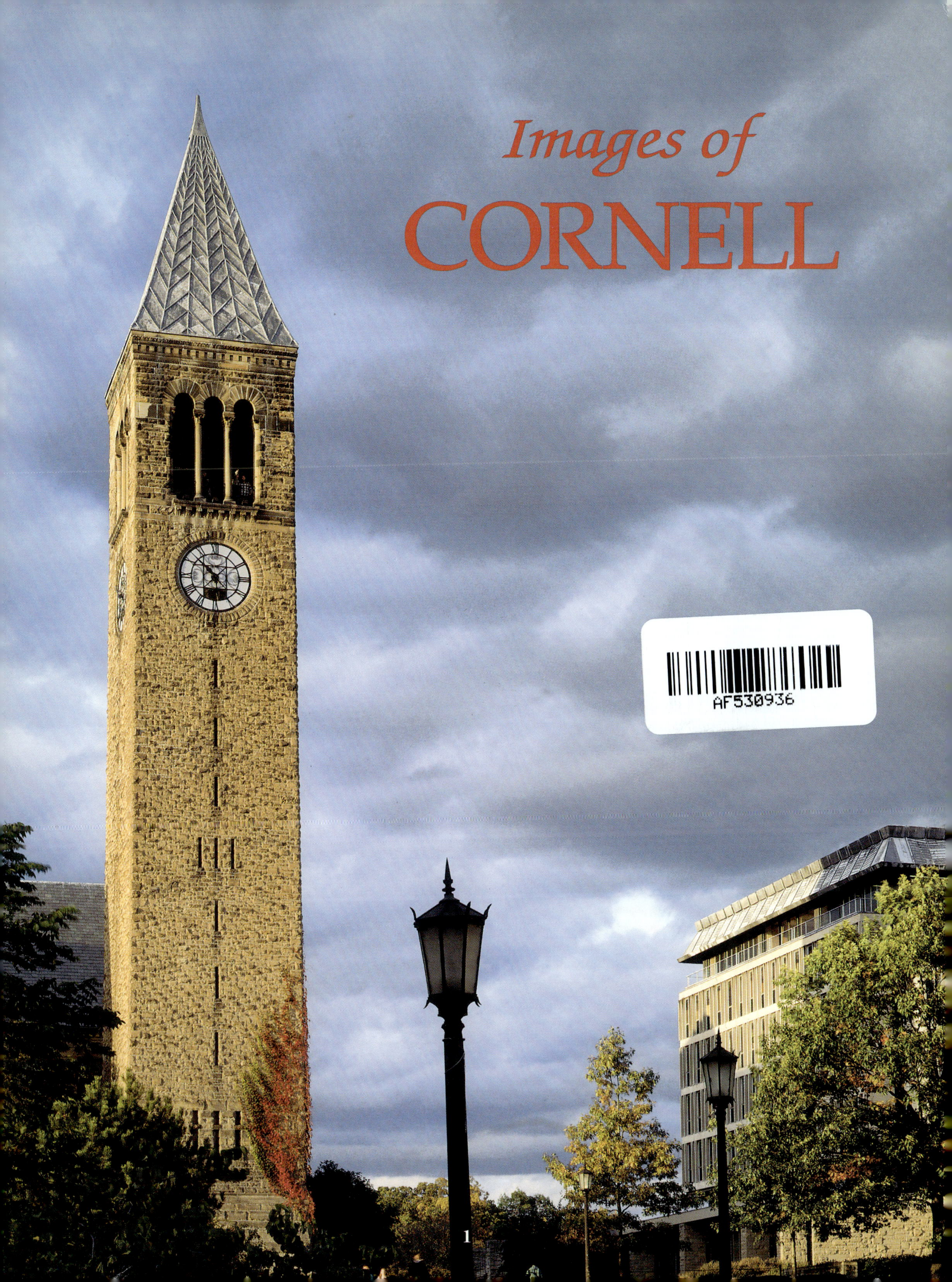
Images of
CORNELL
AF530936

For Melissa —
Hoping this brings back many happy memories of Cornell!
Alan Nyiri

## Images of Cornell

First edition printed in 1999 by the
Cornell Campus Store in association with
I.R.I. Studios, P.O. Box 188, Poultney, VT 05764.

Executive Editor: Emily Gray,
with help from Peggy Haine.

Introduction by President Emeritus Frank H. T. Rhodes.
Design, layout, captions, and editing by Alan Nyiri.
We would like to thank the Cornell University community for
its cooperation and assistance in making this project possible.


Printed in Canada by Dexter Colour Canada.


ISBN 0-9671311-0-3

Melissa '95
with all good wishes
Frank Rhodes

# Introduction
# by Frank H. T. Rhodes
## President Emeritus

Shortly after Cornell University was created, on April 28, 1865, the university's founder Ezra Cornell, his son Alonzo, Francis Miles Finch (a friend who was soon to be Cornell's attorney), and the university's first president, Andrew D. White, set about selecting the site for the new university. They made their way overland, since there was as yet no road, to the top of East Hill. From that vantage point, they could see a shelf of land part way down the hill, and the three younger men quickly agreed that the shelf would be the perfect site for the new university. Only Ezra Cornell demurred.

"Young gentlemen," Cornell said, "you appear to be considering the location of half a dozen buildings, whereas some of you will live to see our campus occupied by fifty buildings and swarming with thousands of students."

Ezra Cornell recommended that the university be built where they stood – on the top of the hill on a line extending from Cascadilla to Fall Creek. Despite his companions' objections, Cornell prevailed, and today his university enjoys one of the most spectacular physical settings in the nation, with magnificent gorges and cascading waterfalls, stately old buildings and impressive modern ones nestled among gardens and green spaces, and with a spectacular view of the City of Ithaca and Cayuga Lake stretching out below.

Ezra Cornell's predictions about the university's potential for growth turned out to be prescient as well. Today Cornell's main campus boasts more than 200 major academic buildings situated on more than 700 acres, and accommodating some 18,600 students, 1,500 faculty members, and 7,500 staff members. Its library, with more than 6 million volumes, 63,000 current periodicals, and a wealth of on-line databases and other resources, ranks consistently among the top dozen or so academic research libraries in the nation. In addition, Cornell operates a medical division in New York City, the New York State Agricultural Experiment Station in Geneva, New York, and several far-flung research and teaching facilities such as the Shoals Marine Laboratory on Appledore Island in the Gulf of Maine, and Arecibo Observatory in Puerto Rico, which it operates for the National Science Foundation.

Through Cornell Cooperative Extension and the university's other extension and outreach activities, Cornell touches every county in the State of New York, and increasingly the nation and the world.

Cornell's distinctiveness transcends its physical attributes, impressive though those are. It was the first American university to offer instruction in practical subjects as well as in the classical studies and liberal arts. It was established, as the land-grant university for the State of New York, through a combination of private philanthropy and public support, an unusual arrangement that continues to this day. In an age when higher education was usually restricted to the privileged few, Cornell opened its doors to students of outstanding ability and promise, regardless of their financial circumstances, and it determined from its founding to offer its programs to women as well as to men and to welcome those of all religious backgrounds, races, and ethnic groups.

Curriculum scholar Frederick Rudolph once observed, "Cornell brought together in creative combination a number of dynamic ideas under circumstances that turned out to be incredibly productive. Andrew D. White, its first president, and Ezra Cornell, who gave it his name, turned out to be the developers of the first American university and therefore the agents of revolutionary curricular reform... Cornell offered nine ways to move toward specific professional careers and five ways to explore: for less, F. W. Woolworth would be remembered as a pioneer in merchandising. The Cornell curriculum brought into imaginative balance the openness of American society, the temporary nature of its directions and opportunities; it multiplied truth into truths, a limited few professions into an endless number of new self-respecting ways of moving into the middle class."

Today Cornell is a learning community

that continues to serve society by educating the leaders of tomorrow and extending the frontiers of knowledge. In keeping with the founding vision of Ezra Cornell, the university fosters personal discovery and growth, nurtures scholarship and creativity across a broad range of common knowledge, and engages men and women from every segment of society in this quest. It seeks understanding beyond the limitations of existing knowledge, ideology, and disciplinary structure. It affirms the value to individuals and society of the cultivation of the human mind and spirit.

This system of values, involving as it does a commitment, not just to personal integrity, but to cooperation, collegiality, and community, is the hallmark of Cornell. It depends upon respect for individual freedom, but also upon acceptance of the responsibility that freedom brings. Historian Carl Becker once observed that Cornell is characterized by the freedom to do exactly as one chooses and the responsibility for whatever it is one chooses to do.

Cornell is more than an Ivy League institution, more than a first-rank research university, more than an institution with highly respected professional programs, more than a flagship center of liberal education and creative arts, although it is all these things. Both public and private in its support, it combines the scholarly stature and sturdy independence of the older private universities with a deep commitment to service embodied in its land-grant status. It is a distinctive university, which occupies a unique niche in American higher education.

It is this blend of characteristics that has produced such remarkable leaders at Cornell. The whole atmosphere of the university generates initiative and responsibility and invites students to accept leadership roles in a host of other areas. Faculty members in its 13 schools and colleges are recognized as world leaders in their fields. A remarkable number have won Nobel Prizes, Pulitzer Prizes, and

**Andrew Dickson White** bust in Uris Library and statue on the Arts Quad.

other major awards, and are members of the prestigious national academies. Cornell's students come from virtually every state in the nation and more than 100 other countries and are among the brightest and most intellectually engaged in the world. Many participate, even as undergraduates, in original research and scholarship and graduate already having presented their findings in a professional journal or at a national scientific meeting.

Over the years, these student leaders have gone on to lead within the larger society. Cornell-trained leaders include U.S. Attorney General Janet Reno, U.S. Supreme Court Justice Ruth Bader Ginsburg, and former U.S. Surgeon General C. Everett Koop; several NASA astronauts; Nobel laureates such as physicists Steven Weinberg and Sheldon Glashow; the late Barbara McClintock, a geneticist; and author Toni Morrison and economist Robert Fogel. They include, as well, leaders of other lands, such as Lee Teng-hui, president of the Republic of China, and leaders of multinational corporations in fields from energy to information technology to finance.

Back in 1965, when Cornell was celebrating its 100th anniversary, Adlai Stevenson came to the campus and reflected on the development of this university and its evolution over the years. "Cornell," he said, "is still dedicated to serving its community, to educating for life, and to encouraging human development in its richest diversity. But the dimension and the scale have now changed. Cornell's community is now the world."

I hope that Alan Nyiri's outstanding photographs will rekindle memories of this glorious campus among Cornell's students, alumni, and friends and inspire a new devotion to the remarkable institution that Ezra Cornell created.

**Morrill Hall**, **McGraw Hall**, the **Johnson Museum of Art**, and **White Hall**

Photo by Andrew Clegg

**Beebe Lake** (below) is a beautiful spot for boating, birding, and jogging. It detains Fall Creek before releasing its waters over **Triphammer Falls** to flow past the old **Hydraulics Lab** (above) and on downstream.

**Fall Creek** (below) continues to carve its way through ancient rock on its journey to Cayuga Lake, over spectacular waterfalls and through deep wooded gorges. In its early years, Cornell supplied all of its own electricity by harnessing this hydropower. Northwest of the campus, the awe-inspiring **Ithaca Falls** (above) is a favorite spot for studying, fishing, and sunbathing.

Opposite: **Cascadilla Creek Gorge**, which cuts through the southern edge of the campus, contains many lovely waterfalls, pools, and cataracts, and rich flora and fauna. Cascadilla Creek has carved the **Giant's Staircase** (center) over thousands of years. The stone-arch bridge (upper right) linking College and Central Avenues was donated by William H. Sage more than 100 years ago. This bridge provides the main entry to the Cornell campus from Collegetown.

Photo courtesy of Cornell University Photography

Fall Creek and Cascadilla Creek eventually empty into **Cayuga Lake**, one of the largest of New York's Finger Lakes. At the southern end of this 41-mile-long lake lies Ithaca, a remarkable city of 30,000 inhabitants who blend small-town life with urbane sophistication. These views of the campus and Cayuga Lake are from the tower of Barton Hall.

Until 1865, the majority of American universities were attended by the sons of wealthy families, who were taught a classical curriculum of Greek and Latin, theology, and mathematics. All of this changed when Ezra Cornell, a self-made inventor and farmer, met Andrew Dickson White, a well-traveled scholar from a well-to-do family. Both men, members of the New York State Senate at the time, shared a dream – to revolutionize higher education and create a fundamentally new kind of university. Cornell would welcome to his university the sons *and* daughters of working Americans from all walks of life, to learn the skills and ideas that would prepare them for thoughtful, useful lives. White wanted a university where students would create their own pathways toward the improvement of humanity through the study of both intellectual and practical courses. Both agreed: "There is needed a truly great university."

Together, Ezra Cornell and A. D. White successfully lobbied for a land-grant institution that would help them create their vision. Cornell donated his 300-acre Ithaca farm and a half-million-dollar endowment; White traveled throughout America, Europe, and Canada to entice noted teachers and talented scholars to join the experimental university. Together, White and Cornell founded an institution destined to become one of the world's great universities.

**Sibley Hall**, one of the university's early buildings, is now home of the College of Architecture, Art, and Planning. Here one can explore the fine arts, urban and regional studies, or architecture and building technologies.

Today, this expansive academic community comprises seven separate but interdependent undergraduate colleges and six graduate and professional schools. The dream of Ezra Cornell to "found an institution where any person can find instruction in any study" has been magnificently realized.

**Martha Van Rensselaer Hall** (right) houses the College of Human Ecology. The college concentrates on studies of human development and society, health and nutrition, public policy, and interior and apparel design. Opened in 1933, the building was named for one of the first women professors at the university (1911), who also was co-director of the Department of Home Economics.

**Goldwin Smith Hall** (below), opened in 1906, is named for an Oxford-educated professor who joined the Cornell faculty at its inception and lectured on the humanities. Today the hall is the center for the College of Arts and Sciences. The strength and depth of its curriculum ranks the college among the top American liberal arts programs. Karl Bitter's statue of A. D. White, in front of the hall, is a very popular campus icon.

**Frank H. T. Rhodes Hall** houses the Cornell Theory Center and other engineering facilities. The College of Engineering is renowned both for its research in major fields of engineering and for its broad undergraduate program that includes study in the arts and humanities.

**Bradfield Hall**, here glowing in rich autumn light, is one of the landmarks of the College of Agriculture and Life Sciences. In addition to housing facilities for meteorology and soil sciences, it features one of the most attractive views of the campus from its top floors.

The impressive Collegiate Gothic styling of **Myron Taylor Hall**, opened in 1930, makes it an ideal home for the Cornell Law School. The building was a gift from Myron C. Taylor (Class of 1894), president of the United States Steel Corporation.

The classic style of **Myron Taylor Hall** is continued throughout its interior. The **Gould Reading Room** is not only an expansive and beautiful example of this, but also a thoroughly modern and functional law library.

One of the oldest buildings on campus, **Sage Hall** (left) was originally built in 1872 as a residential and educational college for women. The original splendid Victorian finial topping the west tower was removed in the 1950s, but a reproduction was installed when the entire building was totally renovated in 1998.

Sage Hall now houses the Samuel Curtis Johnson Graduate School of Management. The renovated and expanded building includes the light-filled and spacious Margaret M. and Charles H. Dyson Atrium (below), a superb site for study and informal gatherings.

**Barnes Hall** was designed by architect William Henry Miller – who also designed Uris Library and its McGraw Tower – and shows the continuity of his design philosophy. Named for New York publishing tycoon Alfred S. Barnes, the 1889 building now contains a recital hall, the University Career Center, and the Public Service Center.

The School of Industrial and Labor Relations applies the social sciences – psychology, sociology, economics, and history – to the study of the workplace. The **ILR Conference Center** (above) faces Garden Avenue. East of Garden Avenue, the **Biotechnology Building** (below) – one of many new high-tech facilities on campus – contains labs for biochemistry and biotechnology, genetics and development, and molecular and cell biology.

The elegant **Statler Hotel** (below) offers guests the latest in hospitality and conference accommodations, and is the perfect teaching facility for students in the School of Hotel Administration to gain hands-on experience. The Hotel School is a recognized world leader in hospitality education and has the largest research library in its field.

In **Peter Plaza**, next to the Statler Hotel, stands the statue ***Herakles in Ithaka I*** (right), created in 1981 by Jason Seley, a Cornell fine-arts faculty member who was also an internationally known sculptor.

Situated on the west boundary of the Ag Quad, **Kennedy and Roberts Halls** (above) house the administrative offices of the College of Agriculture and Life Sciences, and communication, education, Cornell Cooperative Extension, and landscape architecture facilities and programs. Below: Tulips splash a riot of spring color across **Minns Garden** on Tower Road.

The **Veterinary Medical Center** (above) is just one of numerous modern facilities at Cornell devoted to the study of animal science and research. Below: Greenhouses glow in the twilight behind the **Boyce Thompson Institute for Plant Research**; hundreds of acres of Cornell farms, forests, and greenhouses provide "real-life" facilities for agriculture and plant-science students.

**Cornell Plantations** manages more than 3,000 acres of natural areas and 200 acres of on-campus arboretums and botanical gardens. These resources are available for research, education, and the delight of all visitors. Pictured here is the Houston Pond area of the **F. R. Newman Arboretum**.

The display gardens around the A. D. White House offer a perfect island of tranquility in a sometimes hectic academic world. The **Big Red Barn** (left), the original carriage house for the White mansion, is now a graduate-student center, dining facility, and splendid spot for a picnic lunch.

South of the Big Red Barn is the extraordinary **Mary Rockwell Azalea Garden** (below). Each spring, this grotto bursts into a sea of lavender and pink blossoms.

**McGraw Tower and Uris Library** – central Cornell landmarks since their dedication in 1891 – were designed by William Henry Miller, a student in Cornell's first class of architects. The tower, built in honor of Jennie McGraw, was based on the campanile of St. Mark's in Venice.

Andrew D. White donated his 30,000-volume historical library – perhaps the most valuable such private collection in the United States – to Cornell University in 1891. William Henry Miller designed this special baroque-gothic-rococo hall in **Uris Library** to contain it.

**John M. Olin Library** (below) is the hub of the Cornell University Library system. **Kroch Library** (above) was built underground and opened in 1992. Accessed through Olin Library, it houses Cornell's renowned Asia Collections (considered to be the most extensive in the world), the Division of Rare and Manuscript Collections, and the university archives.

Containing more than 3.1 million of Cornell University Library's 6.4 million volumes, **Olin Library** is the largest of the 17 campus library facilities, and one of the largest academic libraries in the United States. Though primarily a resource for researchers and graduate students, Olin also grants broad access to its books, maps, newspapers, microtexts, and specialized electronic services.

Dedicated in 1875, **Sage Chapel** (below) was named for its benefactor, Henry Sage. Because Cornell has been "nonsectarian" since its inception, Sage Chapel has no permanent cleric in charge, and its religious services are conducted by visiting ministers, priests, and rabbis. The magnificent pipe organ (above) was built by G. Donald Harrison and is regarded as one of the best examples of his work.

**Willard Straight Hall** (below), one of the nation's first student unions, was a gift from Dorothy Whitney in 1925 in memory of her husband, Willard Straight, a 1901 architecture graduate. He requested in his will that his estate be used to make Cornell a more livable place for students. These students in the Straight's Browsing Library look very comfortable indeed.

**Schoellkopf Field and "the Crescent"** (below) – funded by the Jacob F. Schoellkopf family, designed by Gavin Hadden, and opened in 1924 – are great facilities for team sports or solitary exercise. The **Field House** (above) includes a gymnasium, strength and conditioning center, and world-class climbing wall measuring 160 by 30 feet. Attached to Lynah Rink – the home of Cornell hockey – the Field House is used for basketball, volleyball, wrestling, fencing, indoor soccer, indoor golf, aerobics, archery, first aid and CPR, and the Cornell Outdoor Education Program.

**Baker Tower** (above), opened in 1916, is part of the west-campus Baker residence hall complex. **Anabel Taylor Hall** (below), given in 1952 by Myron Taylor in memory of his wife, is the last of the great Gothic-style edifices to be built on the Cornell campus. It houses Cornell United Religious Work, which supports interfaith activities.

At the base of Libe Slope (above) stands a handsome cluster of residence halls constructed of native bluestone. Designed to compliment the English Collegiate Gothic style of the nearby Baker complex, **Mennen and Lyon Halls** (at left, below) are linked to **McFaddin Hall** (at right) by the **War Memorial** cloister (center below and opposite), dedicated in 1931.

Cornell's first auditorium, **Bailey Hall** (above), opened in 1913 and was named for Professor Liberty Hyde Bailey, the first dean of the College of Agriculture. The **Center for Theatre Arts** (below), which opened in 1988, provides state-of-the-art facilities for presenting provocative theatre and innovative dance performances.

World-famous architect I. M. Pei designed the **Herbert F. Johnson Museum of Art** building. This singular structure is regarded by many as a work of art in itself. With more than 32,000 works of art spanning 40 centuries and six continents in its permanent collection, the Johnson Museum of Art offers excellent art education programs and is an invaluable cultural resource for both the Cornell and greater Ithaca-area communities.